AF270456

GO DOWN ODAWA WAY

D.A. LOCKHART

KEGEDONCE PRESS, 2021

Published by Kegedonce Press
11 Park Road, Neyaashiinigmiing, ON N0H 2T0
Administration Office/Book Orders: P.O. Box 517, Owen Sound, ON N4K 5R1
www.kegedonce.com

Printed in Canada by Sotek Graphics
Editor: Joanne Arnott
Art Direction: Kateri Akiwenzie-Damm
Design: Chantal Lalonde Design
Author's photo: D.A. Lockhart

Library and Archives Canada Cataloguing in Publication

Title: Go down Odawa way / D.A. Lockhart.
Names: Lockhart, D. A., 1976- author.
Identifiers: Canadiana 20210352361 | ISBN 9781928120315 (softcover)
Subjects: LCGFT: Poetry.
Classification: LCC PS8623.O295 G6 2021 | DDC C811/.6—dc23

For Customer Service/Orders
Tel 1-800-591-6250 Fax 1-800-591-6251
100 Armstrong Ave. Georgetown, ON L7G 5S4
Email: orders@litdistco.ca

We acknowledge the support of the Canada Council for the Arts which last year
invested $20.1 million in writing and publishing throughout Canada.

We would like to acknowledge funding support from the Ontario Arts Council,
an agency of the Government of Ontario.

"Is not the very earth we stand upon built

from the bones of the past?"

– Campbell McGrath

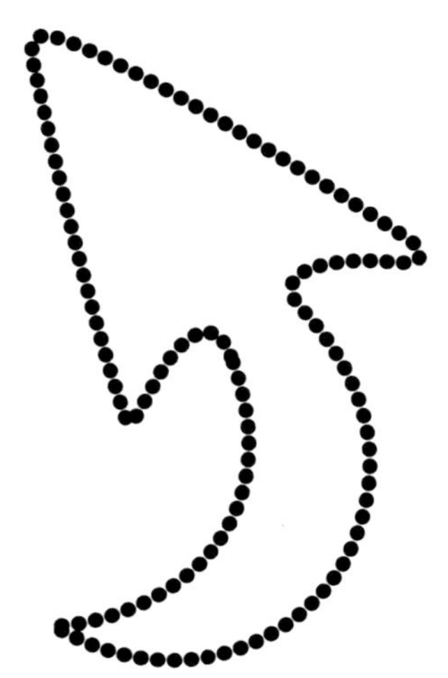

CONTENTS

SÈSKAHTELAHTUNK

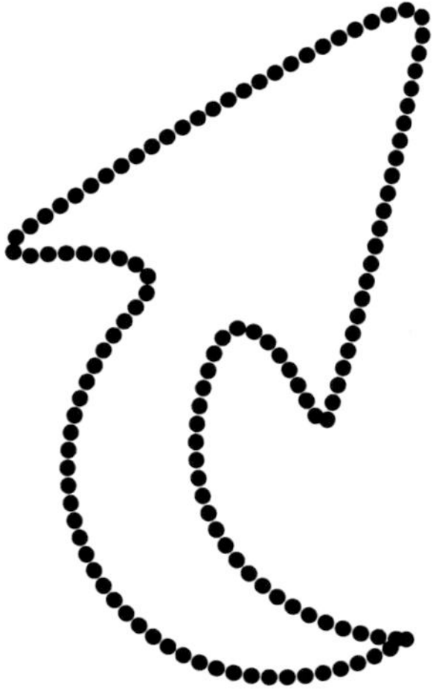

Sèskahtelahtunk

Struck upon stone,
    these words,
    a match,
    shall flare
    to life, and
    from the south,
    breathe the essence,
    the glow
        into tumble
    burn
        of Odawa
        council fires.

Shoreline stone,
    shattered to spark,
        amalgamated
    into sacred fire
    restored
to narrow shores,
once constellations
of ancestral camps.

That our fire
    shall ignite
    the gossamer
        of all
    twelve heavens.
    Be duplicate
    atop waters we
    draw for life itself.

Sing of mpi,
    the multitudes
        carried within,
    of manëtuwàk
        that guide
        their courses,
    of awèn'tëtàk

that dwell along
their bodies,
        smooth
as blue racers
stretched   out
in   full   May   sun.

From the south
        our light shifts
        over   moraines
        of deceased caribou
        to kitutènay, roots
        guided by map makers,
        con-men who fill
        marshes
        with politicians,
        luxury automobiles.

In return we shall pour
        forth asuwakàna,
                our melodies
        into winds
        in Mahtënu fury,
        striking back
        at the world
        we find absent
        in our migrations.
        Spirit of shared
        land, time, being.
        Men   from   far off
        lands, become
                open vessels
                for manitou
        of our shared land.
        Sparks ignited,
                pressurized under the weight
                of a million lineworkers,
        who refused
                the fate afforded
        flyover country.

That this shared breath
shall light
            a midwestern sky of fires.

In song, in light,
        in mighty
        eight hundred megawatts,
        all of it, rain down
                in analog
        UHF vibrancy.
        Baptize us,
                from Black Bottom
                to Depot Town
                to New Gnaddenhütten,
                to Maguaga,
wash away what hides
        our ancestors, our past,
                the essence of our collective.

        For memory
                    of what is lost
        can never be
        recovered;

treaties signed,
                    rivers retreated
        beneath ground,
                lokanahunshi,
        their cooling summer caresses.

Let this be our blues
        our asuwakàna
        our nagamonan
        our guide
        to   walk   the   Odawa   way
        upon this, the land   the sky   the rivers
        before us.

ZHAAWANONG

Through the Grey Survivor Sings of Amimi

Our afternoon cut by the howl
of a red-wing blackbird, shoulder
pointed out in medicine wheel
regalia, a survivor shrill call
through a grey thickening day.

How it sings, like a mile wide,
three-hundred mile long, fourteen-
hour flyover of amimiyok before
settler gun barrels. Men with mouths
open ready to devour creation, take
each of the beating heart mass
by disease, deceit, callous greed.

This stentorian song, rips open
into chatter of sparrows and wrens,
shakes us into a momentary focus
beyond car traffic, the whirr of
air conditioner compressors. Each
holocaust has its survivors, songs,
individuals that remain and call out
to what was taken before. Endure.

Chiskukus Balances Upon a Mimosa Branch

Upon a mimosa branch, chiskukus balances,
serenades old growth shingled roofs, trills.
about rain, distant paths of airliners, cirrus
clouds, venerations for this our urban oasis.

Where Odawa corn fields grew, fences
pause wind and song, and her song stills.
Upon a mimosa branch, chiskukus balances,
serenades old growth shingled roofs, trills.

I wish shaxakwtis songs could silence
cross-traffic at Pillette, note-by-note rebuild
lost marshes, cedar stands, coyote medicine.
We are left in chorus of muffler free trucks.
Upon a mimosa branch, chiskukus balances.

Pipisilunkòn Carve Their Hunger into Creation

Pipisilunkòn carve
figure eights
in sky between
outstretched oak,
maple branches.

Frantic they engulf
fresh hatchling swarms
through each pass
above the side street
of this old whisky town.

Covetous of creation
left to them, they slip
between shadows, silent.
empty sideways and porches
conceal long past roots
of shoreline forests.

Their hunger to survive
snowfalls, green lawn
pesticide applications,
audacious in each loop
connecting to a central
point of sky left to them.

They Gouged the Earth to the River's Edge, Great Western Park, Windsor, ON

The concept must have been
to dig deep into the mound,
past jiibegamig footings,
overthrow the dodem stakes,
scrape the earth of that which
preceded their arrival, didn't
glorify their discovery. Here
the men uncovered them, tossed
them piecemeal into the river
laid down rails and ferry docks,
lowered ground to meet waterline.
Here, waterfront renaturalization
brings bike paths, open grass,
train station turned to bathrooms,
quarried shoreline of rocks
for sturgeon and mink settlers
can lay claim to saving.

Nain Rouge Arrives at Hogg Island

Night comes on strong
in the cold bank of fog
as it rolls upriver past
Hogg Island towards Pontiac's
last camp before Detroit.
Bloody run rests inland, mirrored
by the persistence of taillights,
coils under earth atop salt
veins alongside sewer lines,
the ashes of a once risen
phoenix, now a murder
of waiting saplings.
Upon the water the land
Metastasizes through the grit
of sleep leftover from line work
the residual grime of treating man
as if they were clocks. This earth
knows itself reflected in the glow
of council fires, the movement
of waawaashkeshi. Out here
on the water, the fog bank claws
upstream, scent of putrid whisky
mash cresting in its wake. Know
that medicine follows the river
at will and that hunger is as deep
as pathways we plunge into earth.

Phillip Beaudoin Arrives at Old Sandwich

Confessed years later,
electric blue deer followed
him along each turn,

he arrives before midday
by canoe, drags himself,
ashore with possessions

indicative of his life-lived,
up the old harbour slip,
past gravel mounds, dirt,

chalk, to the no man's land
of Russell Street. Says nothing
of freighter wakes, miles of car-

part construction site deliveries.
Utters nothing about Alkaline
deer, trampled earth, their battles.

Unsettled gaagaagiishibag form
threats like leaping carp. One
man portages his canoe up

South Street, gaze fixed
forward towards Bloomfield
past the shuttered Freshway.

Arrived from the lands
of Splitlog's Wyandotte
nation. His visions not

of Louis Gervais, but creation's
heart beat free in the waxing air
rising from a quick moving river.

Know that Every Lie Begins with Words at Peche Island

In all the ways that places can be
rewritten, understand that this turtle
shell island at the mouth of the little
round lake ignited the Second Fire,
brought three nations into union,
rested the medicine man's dodem
that could deceive no bear, nor possess
the beautiful woman whose spurned
affection caused skies to boil, islands
to be rendered from lake bottom,
inland seas to churn, change course.

Second, in the way no settler words can
gauge remedies in northward winds
through staunch collards, the humour
of settler families and a liquor magnet
deaf to cries of bad medicine thirty
generations in length, proclaiming curses
to a god of indiscriminate small pox deaths,
an artificer of a thousand wars. Yet, speak
not its name beneath the second fire
charcoal, bound by the shards of mussel
shell wampum by which Three Council
fires burned on through multiple millennia.

Still, it burns, not smolders, not flares,
rather slow and defiantly as if with fuel
that knows no end, burns on towards
an Eighth Fire that shall embrace us all
know that curses from bears that failed
to find the love of a woman and raged
like a Hunting moon storm on Superior
so murdered a man in jealousy and broken
tooth agony that this island holds medicine
beyond the word curse, well beyond
the best wishes of hopeful settler fishermen.

Down Seminole after Mania Thirty-Five

Spring descends warm,
heavy in the gaps between
road top dry spots, cars
resting beneath sparse
street lights. Our night
shimmers in watery gauze
that caresses and coaxes
this end of Ford City free
from winter. Warehouse
shines the U-Haul oracle
to utilitarian single and
two-stories below it. Feel
No Ways comes on Detroit
radio, I turn onto Seminole.

Combined skylines rise and
are the constellation I plot
my course homeward post
Wrestlemania Thirty-Five.
Every basement from St. Luke
through Pillette is a vision
of the world seen through
shadow-rimmed red eyes
of looming morning shifts,
knowing that each year
will still bring spring
so long as the last bell
and pinfall happens on cue.

Time's passage measured
in match bells, synchronized
crowd chants and how larger
than life men balance before
them on ropes designed to
contain their ferocity.

Our Council Fires Shall Burn

We live on
          in spite of city
anthropological reports,
          digs
          for lost tools
          and pottery shards
to prove settlers
          are doing right
          by memories of awenik,
sending remains   to
          unceded land
                    to a watershed distant,
we linger in the slow removal
          still at pace   two centuries in.

          Each paper,
                    every shovel-full
of ancestor rich soil
          a glass bead glimmer
          of bureaucratic wishes
that we are
          and remain myth
like shoreline mastodons.

Upon this roundabout land,
          cleared for a tribute
          to a warrior prophet
                    whose words
                    deeds are co-opted
for settler images
          of virgin land
cleared of awenik,
          fought over
          between nations
                    of thieves,

Let us light the fire
          that burns within creation
let it rise
          in mirror through the work
          of our hands.
That it shall burn
          into our collective
industrial night announces
our council's return,
          speak to every way
          we wouldn't leave.

NIINGIDAWITIGWEYAA

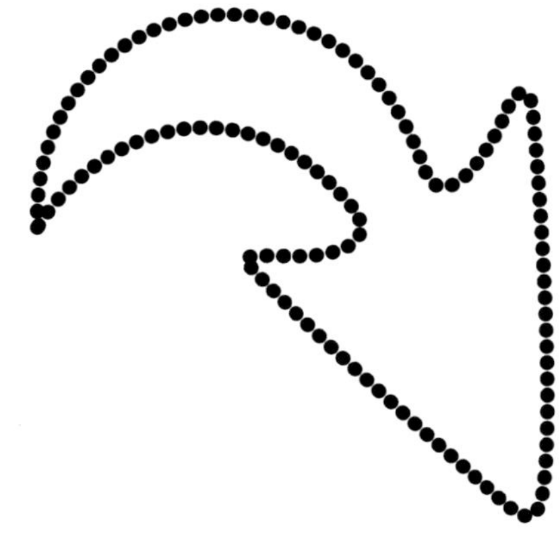

Inland to Niingidawitigweyaa

Plunge, across the wide-open
        Medicine Line
through the Maumee plains
        we ride in sport seat incline
        along paths laid down
        by departed recipients
        of Second Fire givings.

Third gear pulsations
        over Interstates
        Punched over
        gentrified moraines,
        McMansion subdivisions
to inland quiet.

To a midland waabashkiki
where the Grand forks
        into Red Cedar medicine

And namegos sheds stars
        into slow moving water.

Here is rest. Here water moves
        languid-like, as if in thought
        itself searching for how to move
        upon land it has been gifted.

Song Opens Daybreak at River Point Park, Lansing, MI.

Cardinal chatters the world into being
above us, a locust tree branch between
power lines the altar from which song
pours forth into light and fills dense
midland air with heat to burn cold
dew into ever lightening daybreak.

Damp light pushed as if heavy sleep
drawn eyes open to greet this day
Kishelëmùkònk delivers as a gift
in solitary form, where Red Cedar
meets Grand River and the once
slow pooling of waters and forest,
gives way to four cars passing
and the song, each word a hymn
to the places we pass in heavy-eyed
near slumber. World unending opens
before us with each quick note
daylight spins another turtle shell
churn and the waters below push on.

Crow Dances Before the February Snowstorm

Repeat after me: Crow's feathers
are rainbows in the right light, though
snow falls, fills these slim asphalt
streets with a whiteness sure to melt,
we must thank crow for sacrifice;
song scorched to cackle, plume
like the ancestors stretched across
a cloudless Ingham County field.

Repeat aloud, the fire is a gift given
from above. Snow like this happens
only when grandfather wind lingers
too long with grandmother moon,
as that old crow hops from peeled-
paint garage to brittle grey fence,
his dance worthy of a grand entrance
at any Three Fires nation's pow wow

Make it known that his star scape
of feathers and a sweetness of lost
song landed him in the good graces
of creation. At the highpoint of an Oak
street yard in the midst of the night's
local newscast spectacle his three-step
hop and whirl shall bring to heel
the four inches of still rising snow
Wings tucked in tight against cold,
he believes his relations still worth saving.

Old Bhikkhu Throws Smoke to Welcome the Storms

He says that rain is coming
up from the south, in the way
you can't trust it. Camels package
in one hand, other shadowing
the lit prayer half dangling
from his lip. Nods to floods
not so distant and the certainty
that we all need water. Eyes
squinted into creases the shape
of maxkalaniat claws, know he reads
land and sky in manner that hunters
in flight read land beneath them.

Township 4 North Range 2 West

It could start with a need
to place familiar names,
surveyor lines upon forests,
outflows of springs, Odawa
medicine, inland ebb and flow
of bird migrations. Arrives at
the name of Biddle City. Arises
from flood plain that was more
flood than plain. Deposits two
dozen New Yorkers who await
the arrival of a city. Their city.

Here, south of REO town,
patience has brought dry land,
comfort of distance between
trees. In the dull slow glide
of gulls above tree canopy
feel the air heavy, tamed, lazy
like dissipating canoe wake
that followed Hugh Heward
inland to a point near here.

Proclaim this river bank to be
safe of dense aggressive forests,
lay plank roads inland from war
councils, looming hunger,
absent if not forgetful manëtu,

In these brick two stories, know
that this drained marsh rises
from settler governments, follows
with threats of returning to old
ways, prophecies of comets
and shaking ground.

In naming one hides it all,
reshapes this land to mythologies
one builds from theft and hunger.

Midway Between Sparrow and the Capital

Know that salvation rests atop
this Michigan Avenue sidewalk
a midway point between Sparrow
hospital and the capital building,
middling between illness and stubborn
sense that one's words spoken into
the right places lands you anywhere
but the former. In this quiet stretch
of mostly gentrified sidewalk, wind
bends cement planter grasses westward
reception behind the neon cross
is empty, blanched out white, mute
in the time it waits between arrivals.
At blocks end, a brunette in tight fit
work clothes slides metal patio chairs
around the front of the coffee bar.
She quietly sings Fool in the Rain,
as if the spirit of every dead K car
finds its rest in pretty Michiganders.
Her song is met by a full CATA line
55 bus, as it moves with sleek hybrid
electric purr towards the capitol dome.

Through August Haze We Look Inward

Be certain that its origins
lie in the manner settlers
cooked black soil forests
into briquettes and fallow
lots, inputs and outputs
of an economy of the rise,
a motion requiring land
and labour for as long as
it takes to dream a way
out. As the capitol dome
half shows itself through
rusted opaque midday sun
know that in total body
in post-industrial broil
is how we must measure
what follows. Inward,
oblivious to those outside,
those past damage done.

At Water's Edge the Words Come to You

The sound comes with the passage
of water past shoreline, amplifies
in the cascade of liquid creation
not given to coarseness of plate tectonics,
the sound is of consonants and vowels
sliding into rightful positions. *Sipu.*

Enduring softness of breath calling
air, coming to rest, and you hear it
again, in whisper of waterline eddies,
repeated past thirteen generations at flight
from long knives, or patriots, or ICE,
or the words they used to cover sins.

Our words are the way we love, share
the gifts of our mother. These songs
rise to meet us, come from waterways
spilling downgrade. Sit. Hear our roots
returning to us. Mid-afternoon sun
serenaded by words we've carried north.

Pèthakhuweyòk Will Find Their Way to Earth

One understands that the floods
will follow, that distant electric
bursts through clouds will find
path to ground, that this branch
of inland rivers will make want
to breach its course. Long-winged
creatures come like grandfather
in springtime, sniff out tobacco
cold burnt into air. Leaves turnt
up, atavistic branches and trunks
warn of eventual hard descents.
Each prayer, each gift, slow swipe
of water at shoreline, whispering
of women seven generations back
that all appetites must be appeased
the clapping of unseen wings
is the gift creator reminds us ways
never disappear so long as people
remain to receive them, steady in
knowing what follows, buckshot
heavy rain, gentle rise of water,
the sebakwat of trees singing
creation into our world. Each
leaden droplet a pathway that
pèthakhuweyòk rediscovers
their way back to our Earth.

Owashtanong Carries Namegos Overland

Run serpentine through midland hills
past shuttered car part plants, beneath
long neglected bridge ways, soft grass
shores that lead back to small plot
gardens, fire pits, fulfilled promises
of multi-generational home ownership.
Settlers come to a land that forced old
ways from the Odawa people, ignited
three-fires of a nation fresh enough
to greet and chase Iroquois from here.
Through the soft meander, slowed
by fish ladders and long-dead power
plants, witness this slow determination
as creation moves inland. Namegos, sky
as laid out by Nanabush's straight path
to ancestors speckled across vibrating
flesh, traverses bled-through marshes
and straight-shot meanders, each pump
of tail and fin the determination settler
death and arrival means less than each
home built and factory torn down. Though
men claiming dominion will come
to pass like thirteen moons and mark
the folly newcomers bring in belief
that creation would be shaped by them.
Namegos will run inland and the waters,
our waters, shall seep past exposed earth.

Swallows Sing the Night to Sleep at Lansing Station

Here, they disembarked
from points strewn
across a double line
of metal hammered
into wood and laid
across stone, a cincture
of each distant township
tighter to this centre.

They came with light
gauged step across even
cement planks, past wide
open Midwestern barn doors,
took notice of a feeble electric
glow that backlit stained
glass windows, faced up and
into cloud shelves crossed
by the lights strung above
nearby Pere Marquette Street.

Here, they'd come to catch
the detritus of long shifts
in auto plants, the promise
at the edge of university life,
hustle favour from men
fed through an all American
political machine. Tonight
in the reticent approach
of a stale spring storm, empty
upturned lights reflect
a chorus of swallow chatter.

This station, decades shuttered,
awaits no new arrivals, greets
the last light of day scooped
from a drizzle heavy sky. With
rain shall come unseen shoots.

Hear this Melody in the Way You Sigh

In this film
of you walking
through butter cream
streets flushed green
in tree leaf soften
skyline, croon this
night into being,
blue eyes and old
standards rung out
through light post
hiding voices and
quiet our world
bathes us in.

In this film
of you walking
there is only granite
buildings, back lit
for dramatic effect,
emboldening myths
of politicians
and bureaucrats
who oversee care
for people, ensure
the water runs
despite the weight
of heavy metals.

Know that film
ages like all things,
perhaps more slowly
all chemicals, dried
or not, find water
return to life, bleed
back to the places
they shouldn't. You
walking on film
as temporary as wisps

of dandelion seeds
Like you still searching
inland routes, with
an appetite that fails
geography, can only
find fleeting satiation
by a Sinatra refrain
Funny each time
I fall in love
It's always you.

Otto E. Eckert Station Taunts Fire to Grandmother

She rises through
nitrous oxide sunset
greets the Boji Tower,
greets it in persimmon
sky, arrives in the fall
of this late burning sun.

Before her, coiling bolts
of coal cooked air pour forth
into diminishing light,
slip and fade in opaque
wisps. One street over

in a sapling park, several geese
lament the lost Oldsmobile
plant. What song will rise
to greet the final train load
of Powder River Basin earth,
when it arrives to be cooked
up beneath the Eckert Station's
unfiltered bundle of shareholder
ambition, pleasure, ambivalence.

Landmarks, despite their poison
are missed in the absences before
and behind us, their ends the loss
of measures to our traces left
upon creation. Grandmother rises,
her downward fixed gaze rests
       on the steady tumble
             of coal-fired smoke
                feeding a hundred-thousand
                air conditioners.

MPI

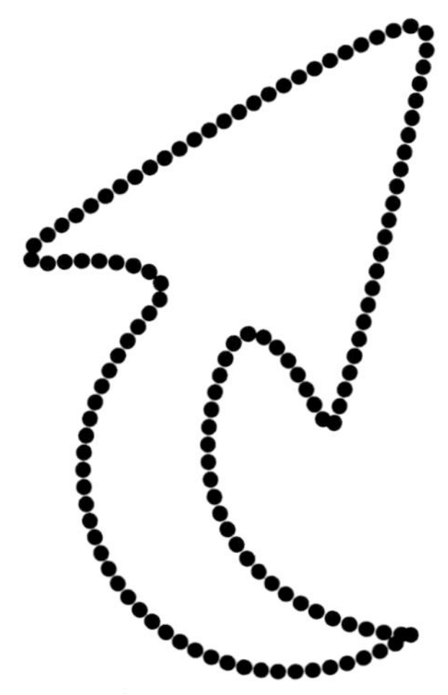

Tëlala Sipu

for the Cedar River

Come through these near still waters,
summer as it hits a tree-frog crescendo
the certain plunge toward sorrel leaves
and decampment songs of migratory
birds. Come to the shore near the full
crescent mound that once surrounded
an inland hamlet. Understand that this
portion of earth, arisen and still rising
from mile-high glacial underbelly
has seen fires, felt human caress atop
soil and grass, warmed by the fires
given them by crows, and embraced
them like tightly woven braids of shoreline
winkimaksko, the ardent citrus of cedar tea.

Chikënëmwi Sipu

for Turkey Creek

Listen as the creek trickles past sugar
maple creek bends, this steady amble
along pressure-treated fences, under salt
bleached overpasses, each current bubble
and twirl a constricted muscle twitch
reaching through manoomin-starved bends.
pushes you downstream along fallow fields
and buried campsites. Know that water finds
ways through creation as it must, drawn by
gravity, as it tumbles downgrade through
emerging subdivisions, past storm drain outlets,
along asphalt concessions. It warbles. It trills.
In song for what is absent, Kuhemena coaxes
this rivulet onward into the great river beyond.

Kwikwinkëm Sipu

for River Canard

Last of the Tiononati Nation retreated
south from here, over the bank to oak
desks of the British Indian Department.
Waters slow like a point at elevation,
but even the prairie horizon, quiet
gentle hints at stillness, each slow drip
enfranchisement that ends bloodlines,
declares that what shall come far
outweighs all that came before. Know
names recede in tongues twisted
with bare-knuckled treaties rather
than the even push of creation itself.
Despite all manner we are called,
land recalls our touch, lingers in wait.

Shëmu Sipu

for Deshkan ziibi

Water moves like a corkscrew
churning soil and rock, leaving
meander and orphaned ponds
where the curvature of water
is simply too strong to continue.
Here, in these bends our world
is rewritten, over words tremble
less in sound, more in connection.
Yet, all of it rests on understanding
that the first gift of creation
is the turtle shell we tread upon.
Water the certain cut of motion
on this land, the divine that leads
us ashore, to places life finds us.

Màxki Sipu

for the Rouge River

I come to you as you squeeze
into the cement culvert bisecting
the heart of Springwells treaty land
at fence line you stretch out
to the horizons, beneath lowrise
office buildings, straight as a slash
of a shixikwe bite, still, as moments
after the strike. Know your destination
arrives at an island of fire, constant
grumble of angry earth. Above us
shopping cart rapids slow to glass
top riffle of water, wailing past
weeds, nènèskakw burst skyward
from cracks in constricting shore.

Nushèmakw Sipu

for the Savoyard River

That asphalt, even when broken,
painted, and patched, is still
unnatural. And it shall break
in face of the down slope road top
from willow tree marsh turned
parking lot behind the old county
building. It bleeds around parking
meters, NO STANDING signs.
Moves like the water it is not. Flows
beneath Congress bound for Fort
and discharge pipes beneath the Lodge.
DDOT 54 sails westward, downriver,
to the great bend of water beyond,
beneath us, water remains water.

Mpiaxkukàk Sipu

for the Clintcn River

Call the water as it bends
like the people our sisters,
brothers of Three Fires
knew the people here to be.
Fork-tongued and rattle
tail tipped, believe that this
water Teflon poisoned,
writhing past suburban brown
fields, unkempt roadways,
has been cooked shallow
bodied by ozone heavy sun.
Pass through here, chased
like our Moravian ancestors
by the persistent hiss of men.

Wisahkim Sipu

for the River Raisin

Here, water seethes by high,
skims the heavy outstretched
tree branches, swollen after
upland dams. Custer lords
over a Subway, back turned
to the river where Roundface
and SplitLog turned American
regulars into wisahkim nutrients.
Here, eastward, the river cuts
defiant past the brick-backed
buildings, boat docks, train
and freeway bridges. Steady,
exhausted in struggle to find
its home in the great lake beyond.

Tànkhanèk Sipu

for Little River

Dragged through still water between
corrugated metal break walls, here
flow is awkward, outward to round lake,
witness of fury from a bear scorned, first
flickers of that second fire, v-shaped
cormorant flights. Inland petro-chemical
lawn cutters and butt rock garage stereos
flesh out this sun-cooked day. Mpiaxkukàk
lay in wait for the first cloud, anticipation
of rainfall that make creation still, linger
for hours over once boiled marsh land
and bless the sun-bleached waterways
enough to rise up, silence the lawnmowers,
radios, deposit silt upon land. We wait.

MAHTËNU

A Drinking Gourd Followed

A drinking gourd followed
leads north to the waters
where the current flows against
an order built by map makers,
a becoming of Up South,
we are the totality of nations
gathered along these crooked
shores. And yet in spirit,
the land calls forth warriors
and from the south they arrive
like Grandmother's nurturing
rain, come to this place
       of industry
       of rebellion,
       of defeat,
       of punishment
       (for the tint of one's skin, numbers
       in one's street address, twang in voice)
       of rebirth
       of promise
       of survival.

A drinking gourd followed
brings our warriors north.

We place faith in our mahtenu,
for we find solace in shared loss.
We find our path in shared victories,
and union in shared mythologies.

Joe Dumars Emerges from Pontiac Assembly

Believe the make of a man
is delivered in a hail of sparks,
stutter step of an assembly
line in full motion. Three shifts
deep and running defiantly day
through night, winter through
to summer. Automation alley
ends in the wide parking lot
outflow around the peach
stone Palace at the edges
of city lights, the last exits
before alien zip codes.
Testify that he arose
not from the South, but
rather rolled off Pontiac
Assembly, traversed M59,
deposited perfect mustached
in the backcourt, engineered
for durability and the squat
rounded strength of Motown

muscle. In motion, each fiber
smooth, like the Cab Calloway
Art Deco flourishes of Baker's
Lounge. Witness how a man
is institution, quiet, steady
in the diesel intake with
free radicals spinning around
each step back basket, every
hard drive lay-up. Baskets,
steadiness of hand, coolness
of form, bedrock to build
and anchor a resurgence story
upon. In emergence, form
behold the spirit of a city
working to be all things
others call common, certain
confidence in each step

that what is being done must
and that work, not reward
is the only surety in life.

James Edwards Clears the Lane Before Scorching Earth

The dream shall always have been
the spin pivot and full shoulder fake
unbalancing the world before you,
before you rise up, fade back, deliver
and sink a shot that silences creation.

So it is, the fourth miracle of Daily
that Buddha himself, broken free
from the third wheel of self-righteous
adoration of humankind, snakes a path
between Trailblazers, drops baskets
as if counted together they claim back

the steady bleed of work from a city.
Believe that this Palace at the far-edge
of the land of Oak, ringed by parking,
and freeways, each fadeaway shot made
by the rental play of a saviour gives
each person something else to yell at
other than Bill Bonds between lawyer ads,
and another reason to believe suffering
isn't the backbone of Midwestern life.

Bill Laimbeer's Fist Announces the 1968 Rebellion Shall Live On

The considered sound,
Bill Laimbeer's fist against
the determined up-turned
cheekbone of a Trailblazer's
center, the only moment,
in violence, in which control
was an asset used to describe
his motions. Fluid in delivery
as if every basket, every dribble,
every straight-legged run down
the court led to that outburst.

Though it is dull, quite quiet
you feel it, radiate upward
to the furthest stretches of Palace
cheap seats, out to dim porch lights
of Pontiac, Allen Park, Warren,
Old English Village, Brightmoor.
Awaken those given to second
or third generations of shift work,

A realization follows in proceeding
quiet: With right leverage, winning
becomes as simple as solid right jab.
Disapproval doesn't mean you
and yours will stay hungry, playing
good guy runs as deep as letting others
take what you want. A well delivered
fist shatters all the ways others forget
about you and yours, reminds them
that what must be had can be taken.

This is the sound of a people pushing
back against the aftermath of a rebellion
two decades earlier, reminding a national
televised audience that swings taken at
heroes from distant cities shall find their mark,

shall tear open a divide that sees only East
and West cities play for the biggest prizes,
ignores gutted neighbourhoods, all-night party
stores, black-mould-painted classrooms, places
each of us directly back in the locus of place
reserved for the Great Midwestern Paris.

Gospel of the Pulled Chair

Wait, in post, for pressure
of a two-and-a-half bill man,
leaned into you, pushing with
all the might of V8 Hemi block.

Slip away, between torque
and release, sliding beneath
basket. And witness descent,
collapse of force meeting nothing.

Anticipation of battle the flaw
that precedes blue collar force
of will and accepts every degree
one must pass to gain what is

not yours. Respect. Fear. Disgust
look received as he hits the floor
beneath you. You hath become
the pulled chair, gospel revealed.

Always remain upon your feet.
Carry the weight of your promises
upon your back. Mahorn. 44.
Pivot when the right weight arrives.

Praise shall follow, sung like snap
of coney dog casings, tang of simple
yellow mustard and sharp onion
bits atop sweetness of white bread.

Despite sweetness this is a city
of sharp edges, a hard shell
that gives way to the steamed
lusciousness of Kowalski meat

slurry, we shall shine in neon
bars of sunlight through full
Faygo bottles, as the prone man
in the wrong golden uniform

from a city that imagines
itself better than the American
Paris crippled since a failed
rebellion, looks up in awe.

Say his name. Derrick Allen
Mahorn. Let it beller down
upon the earth. Say defeated
once, we hit harder, smarter.

Let those ring out and above
triumphant synth rock. Walk
back down the court, prepare
for the next part of your shift.

Not given to flight, nor
to the sweet soft roll of ball
from fingertips. Let it be known
you understand Detroit muscle

when to utilize it, when to
push back, when to struggle,
and most importantly when
to fall back quietly. Wait.

Zeke Carries a City Upon his Back, Falters

He understands, crumpled on
Great Western Forum floor,
that the fight has landed him
here, in the hard moments
that craft legends and men
from simple acts of doing
the work that must be done.

Away from home, coursing
pain from an ankle ruptured,
he thinks little of origins,
instead of the championship
that a city on the decline needs.
Creation pauses beneath lights
cast down by Hollywood, meant
for Magic. And we recall

he arrived like legend
from the depths of Hoosier
backwoods hardcourts, from
the wrong side of the Great
Black Swamp, arrived
as the lustre of the arsenal
of democracy reaches its
least, as global free markets
drained a manufacturing city
to its suburbs, and distance
became measured by state
lines street intersections.

Measured this man is lanky,
but not tall, sweet-faced with
moves like a Jackson Five
vinyl, the middle Lord of Our
Lady of Sorrows comes to us,
delivered by Knight into our
midst. Fiftieth second, he rises.

Returns to the court he knows
that he must claim for a people
watching from afar. First basket
he flies loose-limbed across base
line into the spectators. Each one
that follows a blur of a pain,
numb instinct to follow through
on what must be done. Spin, rise
cut, double clutch, they fall and
the untouchable comes within reach.

He drops twenty-five
in the last twelve minutes
of what needs be the final
game of the season. Stands
tall enough between shots.

The city upon his back,
weight upon just one high
socked leg, Zeke witnesses
the aftermath of abrupt
whistles, network television
pressure as the golden
children are delivered
that which script writers,
advertisers demand. Two
free-throws and white noise
of tens of thousands receiving
what they have come expecting.

Gaze fixed upon hardwood
below, our legend spans arms
across the shoulders of fellow
warriors, leaves through tunnel,
understands that this struggle
knows heroics but no reward.

The Microwave Leans into a Fourteen-Footer

Let us admire then,
these sweat-glistened
monuments to money
earned the hard way,
come by in unlikeliness
of unionized benefits,
hazy nights, half-waking
days, and the forty-five
minutes that divides
people from heroes.

We watch from afar
like Detroit the beautiful
of people of streetcars
or elm-lined trees,
mould-free schools.
Know the wingman
will rise, pull us
from the slumber.

Microwave leans into
Kercey fourteen feet
out, stiffs with a mean
dead arm at a mid-week
Warren Assembly shift
change. The way an
inflated ball launched
through a net can
silence an arena
a continent away
breathe life into
a Midwestern city
on the verge of sleep.

WAAWIIYAATANONG

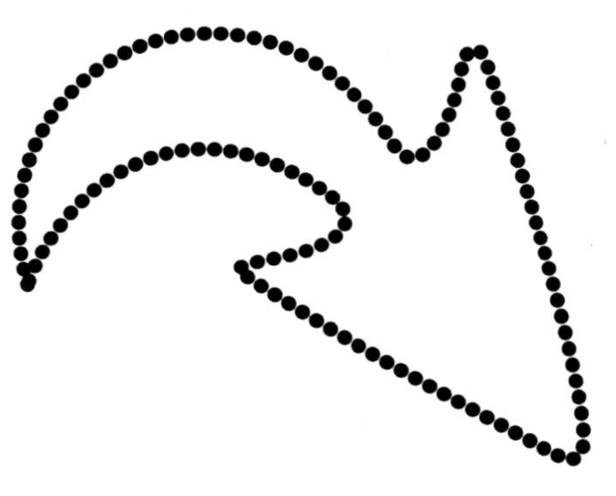

Finding Indigenous Drift Along Hines Park Drive

That time you are
                        slow   rolling
      a lightly used Ford Ranger,
flare side,
                     through
                     the two-lane
                     drainage basin
      of a park.

Bisecting territories
      of fire-dancers
      escapees from Ohio,
the degrees of Heights,
townships   and   county   lines,
slow roll like mpi
we can speak of
      but dare not
      touch.

You understand
      this is how
      a city   on   the   sprawl,
      addicted to cars,
      covering
      distances
they can't own,
      feels its world
                    in drift of   summer   tires
                    on sun-warmed asphalt.

you understand this drift
      is how one connects
to the parts of creation
      obscured
      by roadways,
      subdivisions,
      BP stations.

Sprinkling
  of bikers,
  joggers,
  geese,
  ground hogs,
  make this
  flood plain
  alive.

Drift with the sweep
  of road beneath
  bunkered bridges
  follow the tug
  of rear-wheel
  held steering wheel.

This is what it is
  to be water.
  Encouraged
  in motion
  by the shape
  of land.

moving downgrade,
  steady
 to inland seas.

Feel the land
around you,
seeping by
as it must,
  and this
lightly-used sport-seated
pick-up truck is Indigenous
in ways
  that birchbark canoes
  and flat
  soled moccasins
  never were.

Medicine Song at Telegraph and Joy

Hear me as I proclaim
a medicine song of thanks
to the sun as it rises above
this Telegraph and Joy Road
Coney Island parking lot.

I have seen blue sky paint
patched asphalt the sweetest
shade of discount liquor
before cooking it clear in
a mere hour of unrelentless bath.

I have heard Broken Bells
in Ford truck cab speakers,
calling forth roadside signs,
proclaiming personal injury
lawyers as Motown's soldiers.

I end this song like cicadas gone
wrong, a song of 24-hour dining,
a backlit song of how work begins.
Lie in wait for the first blue cracks
of sky, eat the breakfast burrito.

Hear me as I state to our city,
we look to the sun's daily return
as the dull marker between doing
what we wish, what lies in us
naturally, and what we must.

We Ride atop Xalahputisikaon

Brought to us
      in the second century
      of our colonial era
      we follow these
      concrete gouges
      across earth that
      we are welcome
      to feel through
      the motion of cars.

And in welcome
      wrapped fingers
      feel pressure
      of mostly even
      ground guiding
      tires along new
      rivers, arteries.

We have stilled
      water. Replaced
      memory with rock
      and the medicines
      they bring, crushed
      spread out eight
      car length, webbed
      like a xalahputisikaon.

We are thankful
      in our freedom
      of motion, through
      once-thick forests,
      over long forgotten
      rivers, creeks, marshes.
      We ramble as if
      this shall be
      the order of all things.

We believe it is
> now. Edsel Ford
> Freeway to Aretha
> L Franklin Freeway
> to Walter P Chrysler
> Freeway to the Fisher
> Freeway, we wrap
> our rocks in stories
> of what has been
> changed.

We know xalahputisikaon
> are pathways for
> hunters, those along
> its course are prey
> We fill these
> replacement rivers
> moving between
> strip malls and
> driveways, drive
> thrus, parking lots.

We dance through
> cavalcades
> of tail lights,
> road signs,
> exhaust miasma.
> Driven onward.

At the edges,
> the hunters wait
> feeling vibrations
> through rock,
> we dance
> driven by lustre
> of each strand,
> driven by familiar
> notions of a world
> unchanged, renamed.

Waabishkiigo Gchigami Bleeds Green in the Absence of the Great Black Swamp

In the sheen of water
        green moves
        like dust

through an open light
        living room window
        sun pouring
        into a room
        that wishes
        anything but
        to be seen.

Our vista is of a sick
bed placed before us
in cloudless light and
we believe that land.

Each evergreen particle
        circles each other,
        recites
        the horror
        of gouged
        earth, bathed
        in chemical
        death broth,
        and pushed
        out through
        sun-cooked
        irrigation   ditches   into
        the shallows
        between islands.

Here wounded
land percolates
        in crests
        of waves.

To touch it
let it flow
into your body
is to bring
the sickness
of a hundred
thousand settlers
closer to the heart
that Creator
gifted you.
Flood the last
bit of sovereign
land industrialists,
farmers, bureaucrats
have not managed
to steal. Erie bleeds

green. In it lament
how Maumee camps
        met fire-dances
        and blue-eyed
        Lenape, how
        marshes are
        where creation
        mixes in absence
        of light, produces

Every truth that settler
tradition and naming
        buries in textbook
        colonialism. Wounds
        left by half-truths
        and gouged out earth
        percolate in the waters
        rendered poison by
        way of treaties cobbled
        from men too cowardly
        to fight wars they knew
        they would lose.

The Land We Inhabit Extends to Here

Traffic passes as if the mighty
800 was the only sound stretched
out to four corners of creation
Smokey Robinson, Al Green, Big
Bopper and The Commodores
trumpeted on the slow roll
of settlers too busy chasing
friendly American ass to know
the gentle caresses of earth herself,
how she greets us in every way
those petty customs agents won't.
This land inhabited not by laws
those from afar posit about it
rather by those that arrive here,
find its music, soak in that song.

Here, it's all glow tube lighting
and rotisserie cooked meat. Each
spin of tagine heater wrapped spit
half Prayer for trauma left behind
half promise for fresh land to heal
ancient wounds. In this palace
named for street food an ocean
away, hard gravel-faced man slices
meat atop pita, know this is timeless
as ishkode. Getting by means selling
what the world couldn't force from you.
Living meaning that home begins elsewhere
and the land we inhabit extends to here.

Midtown Iguana

Little registers before
the east-bound departure
of a Tempo,
                              stuffed Iguana
                   perched
                         in rear window,   looking
          at the world hungry.

          The driver, too-tightly collared
shirt, three-day bender scruff
                              with cigarette pointed
                                   outward
                         between two
                         well-positioned
hands on the wheel.

And that Iguana,
          one-time pet,
          sure-fire thrift-store find,
          heirloom,
stares boldly
          into midday sun,
          posture frozen in stride.

Proclaims in bow-
          legged sternness
          creation needs
          to be told
                         one can be
                         strong
                         and
                         eternally
                         famished.

In the Night Understand You Belong Here

That this city should drift
in the dampness of autumn
as if Glen Fry answered
each rock saxophone drone
with a guitar riff akin
to a cardinal calling out
from still full-leaved trees
that that song should
carry people as they walk
from the closing darkness
of clubs and taverns. You
belong to this city. You
belong to this night. You

in the quiet, lustful hours
following last call, ever-
present fear of what light
might burn away, believe
the open street quiet, haunted
by shift-work sedan spectres
in this sleepless city here, on
foot touching a land at rest
Watch your one true love
in deepest slumber, know
you belong to this city.

Springwells Treaty Makers Foresee the Development of the Ford-Wyoming Drive-In

Look up from the plate of half-gone
apple pie at the last Big Boy before
Wyoming turns Michigan Ave from
Dearborn to Detroit. Believe that the
sweetness of the all-American dessert
was the reason White Eyes surrendered
this land beneath us all. Its portioned
out flaky crust and sugary jam filling
provides a portion of our only treaty
annuity this side of the Medicine Line.

For that, be thankful in this neutral
zone of sorts. Same treaty that deposits
a fresh-blooded pale Livingston County
Christian girl for you to drop traditional
Lenape teachings on. Between porcelain
replica mugs of All-American diner coffee,
you aren't sure she understands this. Akin
to the great 1848 Walpole Council, this
council is in passing, two parties certain
of what constitutes sacred. Know this
place is as much hers and it is yours. Yet,
she is convinced in every way about
how creation favours her, how things
like treaties and apple pies and drive-in
movie theatres are gifts for her alone. You

know that Oshawana was right.
In a city built of freeways, understand
there is nothing but the faith and
histories we carry and the places we
talk about reaching one day. Know too,
that you are not here to dissuade her
from her beliefs. This is ritual snag.
Celebrate the sweet buttery pie crust,
how this is the only hunt afforded you
generations that foresaw Farmer Jacks.

As the sun slips beneath the horizon
that Michigan Ave chases all the way
to Apsaloka Territory, leave. Walk on
that land to the Ford that will carry you
across a quarter-mile to an art-deco
parking lot to witness how Americans
dream of what they must look like
to others. How they will blow up
their own cities in car chases that
transform thieves to heroics and reckless
vigilantes. Outliers, the monsters

they lynch dark-skinned men for
rumours of love affairs. As we cross
the threshold from street to parking
lot facing the screen of America's
self-deception, you know to keep eyes
on her and that the greatest fortune
follows those that look the least like
the ancestors. Fire dancers morphed
into distant flashing LED signs,
taillights of passing cars, snap of car
stereo tuning into the latest fantasy.

Gospel of Seger Traversing the Great Black Swamp

Let lightning roll over top farm fields,
shatter open this night christened
by thunder beings. Flash exposing
dried earth alongside two-lane blacktop.

Roll in the gospel singers, that their
chorus of punctuated sweetness shall
lighten the burden of how an aging
man can come to accept memories

of that which will never return. Waiting
on thunder, awoken in night, taken
to cruise southward to the places so
many were forced to surrender to lesser

men. South through the dark sky belt,
once demarcations and porous edges
of marsh large enough to obfuscate
survivors of a stolen confederacy.

State lines that played front lines
to a war between lesser governments
the goal that we drift towards. Carried
by sweet memories of what once was.

Monroe, Tecumseh, Perrysburg,
Luna Pier, Maumee County, look for
and fail to find names of familiar.
We live beneath the banner handed us

from fractured nations, still water.
Move upon the land at speed,
the Gaussian blur pulls what
should be from what is. Roadside

pullouts and mats of phosphate
fed algae appear as fresh carpet
of forest floor, bison prints from
passing herds. Electric hum

of life before Pioneer treated
soybean fields, familiar as
hum before the MC5 break
into a full-throated Dodge

Main holler of Kicking Out
the motherfucking Jams. Follow
it, seek out forests, still water,
oceans of birds. Ain't it funny how

the night moves with autumn
closing in, clouds visible only in
passing and distant lightning, feel
that lighting and wait on thunder.

As you cross before broad mechanical
farm lands, none of this front page
drive-in news, rather footnotes
in the process of reclaiming lost things.

Lost marshes, the lush darkness
between forests, lakes, prairies.
Gene Stratton-Porter, the Miami,
Lenape survivors transmutated

through glyphosate-drenched fields
into state approved reflective
signage, corporate food chains,
an electric hum of ancient lights.

The way that the car cuts township
lines, follows through treeless bean
fields, glances junkyards, leads to
the distant promise of city lights.

All the while the quiet of an empty
backseat, happiness in faded warmth
of a passenger seat emptied a lifetime
ago. Each mile of cleared land declares

Go down Odawa way, guide this sedan
northward to the great bending shores
between lakes larger than seas. Make
front page driving news, arriving along

spider vein freeways. This is home
in the lands warmed in the afterglow
of the second fire of the Midewin
at the bend in shores between mënëpèko

where the medicine songs rain down
from thunderbirds and mpi never forgets,
working and practicing each line, each
verse, each mile declares I remember.

GLOSSARY OF TERMS

The following are terms utilized in the collection taken from Lenape (Southern Unami Dialect/(ul)) and Nishnabemowin. The author has used these terms so as to maintain and build upon key cultural metaphors and in keeping with the need to preserve these critical languages. As the author is Lenape, the traditional term defaults to Unami with Nishnabemowin being utilized where knowledge gaps in the language appear and no suitable non-native linguistic term would suffice. A list of key figures and places that may not be familiar to all readers follows.

amimi/amimiyok – passenger pigeon(s) (*ul*)

asuwakàna – songs (*ul*)

awenik – people (*ul*)

awèn'tëtàk – little people (creatures akin to faeries) (*ul*)

chikënëmwi – turkey (*ul*)

chipayëkan – Skeleton Dance (how the Lenape carried their dead with them after contact) (*ul*)

chiskukus – robin (*ul*)

chulënsàk – birds (*ul*)

gaagaagiishib(ag) – cormorant(s) (*nish*)

Gchi Mkademshkiig – Great Black Swamp (*nish*)

ishkode – fire (*nish*)

jiibegamig – burial house; casket (*nish*)

Kishelëmùkònk – Creator (*ul*)

kitutènay – large city (*ul*)

kwikwinkëm – duck (*ul*)

lokanahunshi – elm tree (*ul*)

mahtënu – bad boys (*ul*)

manëtu – spirit (*ul*)

manëtuwàk – spirits (not of a person, but of the land) (*ul*)

manoomin – wild rice (*nish*)

maxkalaniat – red-tailed hawk (*ul*)

màxki – red (*ul*)

mënëpèko – lakes (*ul*)

mishupishu – underwater panther; mythological protector of copper (*nish*)

mpi – water (*ul*)

mpiaxkukàk – water snakes (*ul*)

nagamonan – a song (*nish*)

namegos – rainbow trout (*nish*)

nènèskakw – red bud tree (*ul*)

niingidawitigweyaa – river forks (*nish*)

ntakiyëmëna – our land

Nuhamena – Our Grandmother (moon) (*ul*)

nushèmakw – willow tree (mother tree) (*ul*)

Owashtanong – Ottawa River (*nish*)

pèthakhuweyòk – Thunderbeings (*ul*)

pipisilunkòn – bat (*ul*)

sebakwat – sound of leaves moving in the wind (*nish*)

sèskahtelahtunk – match (for striking to light fire) (*ul*)

shaxakwtis – tree frogs (*ul*)

shëmu – antler (*ul*)

shixikwe – rattlesnake (*ul*)

sipu – river (*ul*)

tànkhanèk – little creek (*ul*)

tëlala – white cedar (*ul*)

waabashkiki – swamp, marsh (*nish*)

waawaashkeshi – white-tailed deer

winkimakwsko – sweet grass (*ul*)

wisahkim – grapes (*ul*)

xalahputisikaon – spider web (*ul*)

zhaawanong – from the south (*nish*)

KEY FIGURES, EVENTS AND PLACES

Deshkan ziibi – Antler River. Also known as the Thames River that flows through southwestern Ontario.

Louis Gervais (1708-1763) – First settler on the south shore of Waawiiyaatanong.

Kuhemena – Grandmother; in this case, grandmother moon. From Lenape.

Maguaga – Huron/Wyandot village on north shore of Waawiiyatanong. Forcefully sold off through Treaty of Greenfield.

Nanabush – The Ojibwe trickster. Nanapush in Lenape.

Nain Rouge – an evil spirit/demon that resides along the north shore of the Detroit River. Famous in local folklore for being an omen for disaster. French in origin.

New Gnaddenhütten – Lenape village along the Clinton River in Michigan from 1782-1786. Village was moved to Moravian Town/Fairfield along the Thames River in Ontario.

Second Fire of the Midewin – prophecy from the sacred Medicine Society that occurred on contemporary Peche Island in the Detroit River generations before settlers arrived. Led to the Council of the Three Fires that crafted the Three Fires Confederacy.

Oshawana – Elder from Walpole. Warrior from Tecumseh's party. Key speaker at Walpole Debate in 1844. Debate was with Jesuit missionaries over establishment of mission on island and whose god was more powerful.

Splitlog – Chief of Wyandot Nation (d.1838). Fought alongside Roundface and Tecumseh for Indigenous Sovereignty. Fought at Fallen Timbers battle. Fought against the forced sale and termination of the Huron reservation in Waawiiyaatanong.

Spring Wells Treaty – an agreement between the United States and the Wyandot, Delaware, Seneca, Shawnee, Miami, Chippewa, Ottawa, and Potawatomi Native Americans; ending the conflict between the U.S. and these Native Americans that was part of the War of 1812.

White Eyes – Lenape/Delaware chief at Waawiiyaatanong who signed onto the Spring Wells Treaty.

ACKNOWLEDGMENTS

The author would like to thank the Ontario Arts Council and the Canada Council for the Arts for the generous funding to undertake and complete this project. The book in this form would not have been possible without the careful, considered, and professional eye and pen of my dedicated editor Joanne Arnott. An immense gratitude is also extended to the excellent literary journals and anthologies where the following poems first appeared.

"Pèthakhuweyòk Will Find Their Way to Earth" appeared as "Kwèkunilunkònachik Will Find Their Way to Earth" *Waters Deep: A Great Lakes Poetry Anthology* (Split Rock 2018).

"Owashtanong Carries Namegos Overland" *Waters Deep: A Great Lakes Poetry Anthology* (Split Rock 2018).

"East Saginaw Street and the Lansing that Shall Be Yours" *Twyckenham Notes* (Fall 2018).

"Chikënëmwi Sipu" *Belt Magazine* (Fall 2018).

"Kwikwinkëm Sipu" *Belt Magazine* (Fall 2018).

"Hear this Melody in the Way You Sigh" *Windsor Review* (Winter 2019).

"At Water's Edge the Words Come to You" *Windsor Review* (Winter 2019).

"Tankanek Sipu" *Windsor Review* (Winter 2019).

"Tëlala Sipu" *Windsor Review* (Winter 2019).

"Song Opens Daybreak at River Point Park, Lansing, MI" *Windsor Review* (Winter 2019).

"The Land We Inhabit Extends to Here" *Windsor Review* (Winter 2019).

"Our Council Fires Shall Burn" *Voices on the Move Anthology* (Autumn House Press 2020).

"Swallows Sing the Night to Sleep at Lansing Station" *Voices on the Move Anthology* (Autumn House Press 2020).

"Through the Grey Survivor Sings of Amimi" *Grain, Storyteller's Issue*, Summer 2019.

"Bill Laimbeer's Fist Announces the 1968 Rebellion Shall Live On" *Fiddlehead*, Winter 2020.

"Crow Dances Before the February Snowstorm" *Fiddlehead*. Winter 2020.

"Otto E. Eckert Station Taunts Fire to Grandmother" *Watch Your Head*, November 2019.

"Màxki Sipu" *Watch Your Head*, November 2019.

"Midtown Iguana" *Juniper Poetry*, Winter 2020.

"Midway Between Sparrow and the Capital" *peter f yacht club!*, March 2020.

"Zeke Carries a City Upon his Back, Falters" *The /tEmz/ Review*, Issue 12, Summer 2020.

"The Microwave Leans into a Fourteen-Footer" *The /tEmz/ Review*, Issue 12, Summer 2020.

ABOUT THE AUTHOR

D.A. Lockhart is the author of nine books, including *Breaking Right: Stories* (Porcupine's Quill, 2021) and *Tukhone* (Black Moss Press, 2020). His work has appeared in *Best Canadian Poetry in English 2019*, *TriQuarterly*, *ARC Poetry Magazine*, *Grain*, *Belt*, and the *Malahat Review* among many. He is a Turtle Clan member of Eelünaapéewi Lahkéewiit (Lenape), a registered treatied member of the Moravian of the Thames First Nation, and currently resides at the south shore of Waawiiyaatanong (Windsor, ON-Detroit, MI) and Pelee Island. His work has been generously supported by the Ontario Arts Council and the Canada Council for the Arts. He is the publisher at *Urban Farmhouse Press* and poetry editor for the *Windsor Review*.